Naked With My Heart

7 Days to Spiritual Oneness

Devotional

By Ariston C.M.

Copyright © 2020 Ariston C.M.

All rights reserved. No part of this publication may be reproduced, distributed, or transmitted in any form or by any means, including photocopying, recording, or other electronic or mechanical methods, without the prior written permission of the publisher, except in the case of brief quotations, embodied in reviews and certain other non-commercial uses permitted by copyright law.

Published by Midnight Fire Industries Inc.

Dedication

This book is dedicated to Rev. Eddie, my husband, my gift from above. You have been such a blessing to me. Since day one, you told me my life would never be the same, and it hasn't been. You have created the perfect conditions for me to grow. Your love and dedication to me is matchless. Thank you for being everything I want, need and more. May God continue to shine upon you. I love you with every part of me.

Table of Contents

Introduction 1
Day 1 7
Day 2 12
Day 3 15
Day 4 18
Day 5 21
Day 6 24
Day 7 28
Un-boxing God 31
About the Author 33

Introduction

Naked Thought...

Today I woke up optimistic. Today I woke up trusting God to do the bigger things in my life that I cannot do, and that I cannot see. I'm also reminded of one of my favorite Scriptures, Psalms 46:10 "Be still and know that I am God." I know that nothing is out of the reach of God and that I can trust Him to manifest the plans and the vision He has shown me for my life. I do not need to worry, but rather trust. This is the only way my faith can grow. So, I ask myself and you a question as well. What part of your life or your journey have you failed to trust God with? The more important question is, why?

I began my introduction with a "Naked Thought." I know you may be thinking, what is a "Naked Thought?" A naked thought is my raw thoughts uncensored, honest, my most vulnerable self. My book *Naked With My Heart* is a seven-day mini-devotion designed to ignite something in you that you didn't know was there. The beginning of self-discovery and a meaningful relationship with God, a higher power, Christ, our Father, our Creator, the Messiah, Allah, the universe, Jehovah, or whatever name you have ascribed to Him. So many don't know where to start, but you must start somewhere if you are going to get on the right path. God has a purpose and plan for each of us, but most do not believe. Perhaps you have some doubts. It's okay. Most don't see the value that God has placed

Naked With My Heart

upon them. You won't see it with the naked eye until you walk closer with Him. That is when He will begin to manifest Himself within you. Then you will clearly see that He is real and you can begin to trust the things that He is doing in your life. There are so many not living up to that plan because they don't know how. The church can teach you, you can fellowship, you can hear everyone's stories, but until you develop a meaningful relationship with Christ, in my opinion, it will all mean nothing. Why? Because you have not experienced Him the way you should. You must experience Him for yourself, in new and exciting ways that let you know that He is real. The only way you will find that out is when you position yourself and allow Him to draw near to you.

Learning to walk with God is not a perfect walk and you will indeed fail many times, but God's grace and mercy is abundant. What is grace? Grace is what you don't deserve, but God gives it to you anyway. A good example of this is favor. What is mercy? Mercy is what you deserve, but God saves you from judgement. He covers it. An example is escaping punishment for a crime you committed. He can carry all of your flaws and everything imperfect about you. Nothing you do surprises Him. You have not done something so bad that He will not receive you in His arms with love. So free your minds. Although you may have sinned many sins, you are made in God's image and likeness and He loves you oh so very much. Give yourself to Him just as you are and watch the transformation that will take place in your life. I promise it will be well worth it. By the end of this devotional, something great will have taken place in your life if you have properly applied yourself. You should feel strengthened, more encouraged, and ready to begin a new life, one with greater meaning. It's okay to begin again, no matter what age you are and what place you are in spiritually. We all can benefit from starting over.

Acknowledging that you need something from God is the first step in entering a relationship of oneness. I believe this is the only way you can begin. Some leaders caution against going to God with a list of requests. I believe we should present those needs before Him and allow Him to sort through our list. It is a common misconception that we need to be presentable before we can enter into His presence. Nothing can be further from the truth. It is when we come to God naked, with a heavy heart, ready to surrender, that He can work best. "The Lord is close to the brokenhearted and saves those who are crushed in spirit" *Psalms 34:18 NIV*. You may ask why? At the point when we have reached the end of ourselves, we find ourselves in need of something extraordinary. It is at this moment that we relinquish the rights of our life in exchange for Him. While this is not typical of everyone, I believe we can all agree that at some point in our lives we have reached despairing moments, such as a major shift in life. A divorce, a sudden death, loss of job, even a deferred dream. Regardless of your beliefs, you have asked for help from someone or perhaps something. For believers, we have looked to God.

Prayer is pertinent in achieving spiritual oneness, it connects us to God. Through prayer we form intimacy by emptying ourselves. In return we may receive correction, wisdom, knowledge, understanding, or healing. Prayer keeps us balanced, by being in tune with the spirit. It often keeps us from

Naked With My Heart

traveling down a path that we were not meant to be on. Prayer protects and it preserves.

I chose to be creative with my prayers, realizing that you can't hold God to one specific way of being or doing things. For example, God will sometime speak to me through symbolism. One day I was driving down the street, the same street I drive down every day. On this particular day, there was a huge golden yellow tree that I had not previously seen. As I approached the tree, it was a feeling that came over me that I have never felt before. God was speaking to me and He let me know this tree was a representation of who I am. It was unique, the only one like it. It was bright, big, and bold. The Lord let me know what He has for me was exclusive. It was a plan that no one could carry out but me. My eyes were open wide and my heart was filled with joy. That day was different for me, it gave me strength and something to work toward. I was able to take a picture of it. However, when I went back to find it months later, even the next season, it was not there. I had a picture of it and I went to the exact location. I couldn't find it. I know it sounds strange, but God wanted me to understand something that day, and I did. I only have a picture to remind me and I will never forget.

The truth is we cannot predict in what way God will move and what method He will use. Isaiah 55:8 says, "For My thoughts are not your thoughts, neither are your ways My ways." Therefore, I created water prayers. Water prayers are a different way of connecting with God. It offers an alternative way of offering up prayers. Most of us drink water every day. Water signifies so many things; for me it means purity, life, and rejuvenation. I desire to have a pure heart and mind, this is the only way I feel I can serve God. I drink bottled water. While I was writing this book, I wrote on my bottle a one word or a one sentence prayer using a permanent marker. Every time I drank the water, it reminded me of what I am believing God for. It also reminded me to pray, even if I am just repeating the prayer on the bottle. During my seven days of spiritual oneness, I drank about four bottles of water per day. Each bottle contained a different prayer. I didn't drink anything else but water for those days. It is something about the prayer being on the bottle and you focusing on it as you drink the water. Something wonderful happens, you are believing God for something you so desperately need. He is the living water and you are drinking it, and symbolically you are becoming one with Him. You are allowing Him to dwell within you.

I am inviting you on this journey. I'm sure it's a different way of prayer, one that you are not used to. The beautiful part of it all is that you don't have to be perfect! There is a reason you are acknowledging that you need Him. You are saying to Him, "I know I'm not what I should be, but I'm trusting you to make me into what you want me to be." For each person the prayers will be different. There is no right or wrong way to pray. God knows your heart and He knows what you stand in need of. You only can give Him what you have. People think prayer has to be fancy and well thought out. It doesn't. It's an informal honest conversation with your Father, someone who loves and cares about you so deeply. He is waiting for you!

The devotion is meant to cover seven days. Each day contains a "Naked Thought" or "Reflection." These are my personal, raw,

Naked With My Heart

or "Naked" thoughts. After my thought, I will list my mindset exercise that I did. This is a process to recondition your mind to think positive. You have to start small and be consistent. You may notice that I refer to my "Replacement Thought." This is what I have termed "Thought Trading," trading a negative thought for a positive one. For example, changing *"I can't"* to *"I can."* Once you trade one thought for another, you can't have it back. You have to repeat it often until the negative thought no longer exist. Don't worry, it takes time and discipline. Then I list my "Water Prayer For Life." This is the prayer that I wrote on my water bottle and focused on for the day. I now have the pre-labeled prayer water bottles and individual prayer labels available on my website. I think you will most benefit if you drink only water throughout the day with your meals, especially if you don't drink water regularly. If you prefer to use a reusable bottle, just use masking tape and a permanent marker. Each day is designed for you to mimic my devotion. So you will write down a naked thought or reflection, followed by a mindset exercise or intimate moment, and lastly your water prayer. This is getting you in the habit of spending time with God. You will develop your own style as time goes on, but I wanted to give you something simple, a place to start. You can modify and change things according to your needs. By the end of the seven days you should feel empowered, encouraged, and ready to plan for what's next. While change is a good thing, it can be full of fear. God will be with you every step of the way, and I will be there too. You got this, you have a brightness that needs to shine!

Day 1

Naked Thoughts:

"Today is a beautiful mild day. I awoke to thoughts of what it would be like if life were exactly what I thought it should be. If it were like I think it should be, where would I get my strength from and learn how to grow? How many lessons would I miss out on if everything was perfect? Would I have the relationship that I have now with the Almighty, if everything went according to my plan? The human side of us wants everything to be right in our eyes, we don't want to suffer, but is our suffering a part of the plan? I concluded that regardless of what I think, I believe my life is what it should be in this very moment; and I shouldn't wish it to be anything but what it is. Today I am able to acknowledge that I need something from God. Will He give me what I think I need, or will he give me what He wants me to have? As I see it, I will always need something from God. Just when I thought I've arrived at a place of independence, I'm reminded that I am interdependent on God. I can rest in His presence knowing that He has my best interest at heart."

Present Day Update

I wrote this book in seven days so that I could give an accurate account of my thoughts, feelings, and progress, although my Day 1 *Naked Thought* was from a year ago. The following three paragraphs were written today, exactly one year after my first *Naked Thought*. Day 1 is the only part that shows a current account of where I am. Keep this in mind as you read the next six days.

As I read my *Naked Thought*, I am reminded of my favorite scripture, Proverbs 3:5-6 NIV, *"Trust in the Lord with all your heart and lean not on your own understanding; in all your ways submit to Him, and He will make your paths straight."* I have seen so much change in my life. I am finally married. God sent me His best, a beautiful man of God. He is a Pastor from Ghana. It's a beautiful thing to see God manifest His promises. I am at peace with the decisions that God has made about my life. I find myself in a place of total trust in God. He has called me to a higher place in Him. A place where I must dedicate everything I have and am to Him. I've walked away from my business and any ideas or ventures that I have concocted on my own and have completely surrendered everything to Him. God is in heavy pursuit of me and I am in heavy pursuit of Him. I'm excited to see what will happen when we collide. I know it will be powerful, because it already has been up until this point. This was not an easy task, as it meant I had to rely on Him to supply my needs, give me direction, and provide confirmation to keep me encouraged on my journey.

The Power of Praise

This week I have been practicing a posture of praise. The posture of praise is intentional. When thoughts arise concerning negative situations, regrets, or anything that will bring you to a low place in your life, you have the mindset to praise God. You begin to just thank Him that it's not worse, thank Him that you are still standing. It's a heart of thankfulness and gratitude focusing on the things that are good. You will find the heaviness that you were experiencing begin to lift as a result of praise. Instead of me praying and asking God for things, even though they were needed, I offered up my praise instead. There were many thoughts and situations that arose in my life. As soon as they happened or crossed my mind, I began to praise God. It was a deep and meaningful praise, one that blessed my soul and set me free. I encourage you to try it, you will gain something very beautiful. Peace that passes all understanding

Initially, when I began to praise it didn't seem like much. The more I praised, the more God began to draw near to me. The praise became deep and I allowed myself to cry and be free in Him. It was meaningful because He met me in a place that was dark, yet I found the strength to praise. God already knows what you and I stand in need of. I had to learn to trust that He will take care of me. Not just me, but you too. All He needs is your obedience and praise. This is something that does not happen overnight. God has brought me to a beautiful place in Him where I could trust doing this. All the work He is doing is on the inside. What's stopping you?

None of my praise manifested in money coming or opportunities, but my inner man is stronger and more prepared on the inside. I understand things a little clearer. If my foundation on the inside, which is the work, beliefs, and promises of God, is not strong, when the storm comes, I would not be prepared. This holds true for you too. Think about your life, the troubles you have faced. Did you face them in your own strength with human knowledge and wisdom? You may find

Naked With My Heart

that you couldn't handle it properly because your foundation wasn't built well. You'll find yourself not knowing what to do. There is so much I have learned. How to have patience, how to be still, and how to let God lead without occasionally stepping in front of Him. These are essential things needed before you and I can advance to the next level. The beautiful part is finally, I'm not afraid to trust Him. You shouldn't be afraid either.

My Water Prayers: "Direction during my transition," and "Acceptance."

My Mindset Exercise: Get a good Scripture or quote and hold on tight.

What are your Naked Thoughts or reflection?

_____

_____

_____

_____

_____

_____

Ariston C.M

Intimate Moment: Write down a fearful part of your journey that you have not given to God. Also, write the reason you are having trouble trusting Him with it.

_____

_____

_____

_____

_____

Water Prayer:

_____

_____

Day 2

Naked Reflection

"This morning as I woke up my heart was heavy and in need of God. I am in a desolate place. I know He is the only one that is able to deliver me out of the bondage that I am in. My life, although it's progressing, is not what it should be. I am in the midst of financial ruin and it seems as though all the walls are closing in on me. It's getting harder and harder for me to breathe. All I can do is call upon Jesus, because He is the only one that can help me. I have to trust Him, He has never failed me yet. It is hard when you look at all the situations surrounding you and you are not sure how you will get out. For me, I have to focus on where I came from and how He has kept me so that I don't resort back to toxic thoughts. I know that I will be okay, I just have to trust Him in the darkness."

Intimacy

Intimacy with Christ is a beautiful thing, but you must pursue Him. What is intimacy with Christ? Intimacy with Christ is a connectedness, a contentment, a love that you will never find in a human. It's your most vulnerable place, but you allow God to occupy it. He knows how to love you in a way that can make you feel most adored, even though you can't quite put it into words. He creates many opportunities for us to connect with Him, but often we ignore that still, small voice. One of the ways in which we developed this intimacy is through relationship. This relationship is formed through prayer. Prayer is nothing more than a conversation with God. There are many different ways to pray. Sometimes you won't have the words, just know that He interprets the way you feel and that is a prayer as well. Scripture tells us, *"In the same way, the Spirit helps us in our weaknesses. We do not know what we ought to pray for, but the Spirit Himself intercedes for us through wordless groans."* Romans 8:26 NIV.

My Water Prayer: For God to move in a mighty way.

My Mindset Exercise: Destructive thought: I am never going to be any more than I am.

Replacement Thought: I am more than enough, and I can achieve greater things as long as I work hard and am diligent in the things that I do. (*repeat daily and often*)

What is your Naked Thought or reflection? Allow yourself to be honest, it's okay...

_____

_____

_____

_____

Naked With My Heart

Mindset Exercise: You can create a replacement thought for your destructive thought or you can choose intimacy and tell God what you need from Him. Be encouraged, He is near.

_____

_____

_____

_____

_____

_____

Water Prayer:

_____

_____

Day 3

Naked Thought

"This morning I woke up to unfavorable circumstances. This is not the best way to start the day off, especially at 6 a.m. I had a choice to make. I could allow my circumstances to overtake me and be disturbed all day, or I could acknowledge it and understand there is not much I can do about it today. I chose the latter and therefore decided to allow the Joy of the Lord to reign deep within. You may ask, how did I do that? I made a conscious decision to try something different. I decided to focus on the Joy of the Lord. There are so many good things that God has done and we so often take them for granted. Today I focused on what I could change. Although I couldn't change the circumstance, I could change the way I thought about it. I could change the attention I gave to it and I did. I know that He has a purpose for the things He allows. I just have to be patient until my change comes. I am so happy that I am able to have peace and joy in the midst of wearisome circumstances. God is indeed faithful."

"The righteous person may have many troubles, but the LORD delivers him from them all; He protects all his bones, not one of them will be broken." Psalms 34:19-20 NIV

The Naked Truth

So far you have spent three days with God. By now you should be in a somewhat comfortable position to now acknowledge the things that are going on in your life, mind, and spirit. This is not an easy task, but a necessary one if you truly want change to take place in your life. This is a part of the reconstruction phase, where you are emptying everything in preparation for the new things that are to come. It all begins with the mind. The more you speak life into something, the more it will grow and manifest. Don't be afraid. Often when you make a decision to move closer to God, your foundation may be disturbed. It's a part of the process. Don't abandon your post, be still and trust. Trust God and trust the process. When we trust God, we rely on Him to move accordingly and in step with His plans for our life. We trust Him to do what's in our best interest. We give up the notion of knowing and trusting in ourselves and our human ability in exchange for trusting in our Creator.

My Mindset Exercise: Wait one day before making any decision. Hasty decisions can be costly.

My Water Prayer: Help me to let go and trust You.

Ariston C.M

What is your Naked Thought or reflection?

_____

_____

_____

_____

Intimate Moment: What will you surrender? You are trying to hold on to something, you need to let it go. It is poisoning you and killing you slowly. It's causing you harm and keeping you in a defeated state of mind. It's crippling your ability to move forward in your life. So, I ask again, what will you surrender today?

_____

_____

_____

_____

Water Prayer:

_____

_____

Day 4

Naked Reflection

"Today I woke up and decided I was not going to be bound by fear and it is past time to change. There are so many things in my life that I have fears about. One of them is being in a relationship. I have had so many fails that I stay guarded in every situation. I am learning that I have to trust God with the bigger things. I have to listen for that still, small voice that sends warnings that we too often ignore. I have decided that I am going to let someone love me, but only according to the plan and purpose God has set forth. Meaning God has given me instructions on the one who will love me and I can't steer away from that. Failure to do so will result in unnecessary pain caused by a situation that I have created. I can no longer allow fear to be the captain of my life. I can't worry about what may happen. The only thing I can do is stay on course to the best of my ability and allow God to lead me to the place I need to be. I know that I can trust God not to allow me to be in a situation that there is no way out of. I cannot change if I don't embrace a new way of thinking or handling of a situation. Change requires action and it begins with your thoughts."

"Do not conform to the pattern of this world, but be transformed by the renewing of your mind. Then you will be able to test and approve what God's will is — His good, pleasing, and perfect will." Romans 12:2 NIV.

Extra Encouragement

You have to begin to live out the change that you want to see in your life. That doesn't mean ignoring your circumstances, but figuring out a way to live beyond them. In my naked reflection, I woke up trusting God for the bigger things in my life, the things that I cannot do and cannot see. *Hebrews 11:1* says, *"Now faith is the substance of things hoped for, the evidence of things not seen."* This is faith, believing God for something you can't see, understand, or even comprehend. Whatever your situation is, you have to try to exercise faith. Notice I said try. All progress is good progress, no matter how small. In the immediate, you are not able to change it; however, you can change the way you think about it and the life you continue to breathe into it. Today is a new day. Are you going to allow your problems consume you? Sort through the issue and even if you can't change anything about it, have a positive mindset about it. Trust that it will work out. I am sure there have been situations that you thought were impossible, but now that you are on the other side of it, you can see that it has all worked out. Think positive, know that it is going to be okay and worrying about it won't change it.

My Intimate Moment: Practicing staying in God's presence and being aware and able to sense it.

My Water Prayer: Prepare me for change *(Awareness and strength to let go of negative things in my life so I can grow).*

Naked With My Heart

What is your Naked Thought or reflection?

_____

_____

_____

_____

_____

Mindset exercise: Who are you? Ask God to show you. Write down three things you want to change in your life.

1._____

2._____

3._____

Water Prayer:

_____

_____

Day 5

Naked Reflection

"Now faith is the substance of things hoped for, the evidence of things not seen" Hebrews 11:1 NIV. Without faith it is impossible to please God. Why? We are trusting a being that we cannot see, control, or comprehend. Believing in Him alone is faith. I thought of the many things that we put our faith in without realizing it. Some situations in our life are automatic faith. Take, for example, driving down the road. We have faith that the person in front of us is not going to suddenly slam on their brakes and cause an accident. We have faith in our interactions with people who come into our homes and provide services. We have faith that everything is going to work the way it should when a human person that we can see is involved. This is our hope, but I feel this type of thinking is incorrect. I'm sure you can look back on your life and see where you have been failed by others. I know I have on multiple occasions. So why are we so comfortable trusting? We have witnessed phenomena and have seen medical miracles, yet we do not trust God. I know I have experienced the work of God in my life multiple times. I have no choice but to trust Him.

Faith

Faith is an important part of your journey. Faith is what allows you to grow into a mutual trust relationship with the Almighty. Without faith you cannot access God in His

Naked With My Heart

fullness. Why? Because you don't trust Him. If you don't trust Him, you cannot allow Him to work effectively in your life. Having faith in God takes time. It takes situations happening in your life in order for you to have faith, trust, and allow growth. God understands what He is requiring of us, especially if we are new believers. We are still trying to make sense of everything. Trusting in something you cannot see or touch takes time. *"And without faith it is impossible to please God, because anyone who comes to Him must believe that He exists and that He rewards those who earnestly seek Him." Hebrews 11:6 NIV*

My Mindset exercise: Write down faith affirmations on note cards and hang them on a mirror or in your room.

My Water Prayer: Trust and confirmation.

What is your Naked Thought or reflection?

_____

_____

_____

_____

_____

_____

Ariston C.M

Mindset Exercise: Write down what you are believing God for. Next, find an object, something small (a ribbon, gemstone, coin), something symbolic to carry with you as a reminder to trust God and have faith in Him. Trust Him throughout your day with the situation, thoughts you encounter, or whatever else you are trusting Him with. You can always use my above affirmation activity if it's easier.

_____

_____

_____

_____

_____

_____

Water Prayer:

_____

_____

Day 6

Naked Reflection

"Today I have a sense of fullness. I am in the state where I am ready to receive. I have prepared myself for a time such as this. Conditioning my heart and mind, ready to receive instructions, vision, and clarity from God. I'm realizing it's only when you have emptied yourself that you are ready to receive. While I have asked for many things, I am open to what God wants to do in my life. That doesn't mean that I will agree fully, but I know if He is giving me instruction then I can trust it." The Scripture says, *"Guide me in your truth and teach me, for you are God my Savior, and my hope is in you all day long."* Psalms 25:5 NIV

Naked Truth

We don't have the capability of seeing our life in its entirety. We don't know how the decisions we will make will affect our future, both good and bad. This is one of the main reasons we seek God. The situation may appear safe. While that may be the case, it may lead us down a different path. I'll take, for instance, buying a house. Clearly, there is nothing wrong with purchasing a new house, it's necessary and it's safe. I had a friend that was looking for a house and she began to seek God about it. She walked in several houses, and although those houses were nice, she was confident that God told her not to get those houses. Initially, she couldn't understand it and was upset because she had found what she was looking for. She decided to listen to God and get the house that He told her to get. It was nice, but it was not like the others. A few months after purchasing the house, a hurricane hit. All three of the houses that she was looking at were destroyed. Had she not listened to God, she would have lost things that insurance couldn't replace. Sometimes we think because it's a house or car that we can make the decision on our own, not understanding we can't see what's down the road for us.

One of the things we must understand is that God's timing is not the same as ours. He will not move when we think He should move, but when it's the proper time. Many of us have a difficult time with being still. To be still before God means to wait, it means don't make any big or hasty decisions. When we are still, we quiet our heart, mind, and outside influence in expectation of hearing from God and receiving direction. What we don't understand is failure to wait costs us and delays the things that He has set forth in our lives. In the end, we will live an empty life and never receive God in His fullness or the things that He has promised. *"For my thoughts are not your thoughts, neither are your ways My ways, declares the Lord." Isaiah 55:8 NIV*

My Intimate Moment: Today I will listen for Him.

My Water Prayer: Fine tune my ears to hear you, oh Lord.

Naked With My Heart

What is your Naked Thought or reflection?

_____

_____

_____

_____

_____

_____

Intimate Moment: Today, remain open. Quiet your inner self and receive what God has for you or the direction in which God is moving you. Perhaps there is a decision you must make. Maybe He is telling you to do something. Perhaps He is speaking through another person or making you uncomfortable in your present place. He's speaking. It may be through a person, something you've read, or a subtle thought that grows. Write down what you think He is saying to you.

_____

_____

_____

_____

Ariston C.M

Water Prayer:

_____

_____

If you find yourself in the state of confusion, know that God doesn't confuse us, He has no reason to. That is your inner self battling. It's okay not to make a hard decision today, God already knows your situation and the timeframe. He passes up many chances to be early, but He's always on time.

Day 7

Naked Thought

My thought today was a prayer. As much as I believe that I have gotten past certain habits and destructive thoughts, every so often I am reminded of them. If I don't work hard to maintain and stay in the Spirit, I will fall victim to those self-defeating negative thoughts. You can't entertain it. You must starve it out by not giving any attention to it with thoughts or words, and definitely not actions. Just because something gets your attention doesn't mean it deserves it. Two Scriptures came to mind, "So I say walk by the Spirit and you will not gratify the desires of the flesh." Galatians 5:16 NIV What does this look like in my life? Remaining in a constant state of prayer, praise, and meditation about the things of God. The other Scripture that resonates with me is, "The tongue has the power of life and death, and those who love it will eat its fruit." Proverbs 18:21 NIV You have to be very careful with your words. They have life and will often take you by surprise..

Intimate Moment

It's okay to be honest, especially with yourself. Everyone you look at has a problem. It may be similar to yours, it may be better or worse. You are not helping yourself by concealing your problem. Things have a way of leaking out when you least expect it. You may think you have solved your problem with anger, only to find out that someone has said something to trigger something in you. Perhaps someone said you didn't have the ability to do a task, start a business, or stop a habit. When they said this, it caused you to blow up on the inside. For some it caused an outward reaction. Those words may have triggered something that was said to you in your childhood. It caused a reaction that you thought you had under control. Now you see it's still an issue. "Naked with my heart" is you laying bare before God, coming to Him with all your bumps, bruises, flaws, insecurities, and everything else that keep you from receiving His goodness, healing, strength, and blessings. You need to see who you are so that you can change. Ask God to show you.

My Mindset Exercise: I acknowledge my thoughts because they are there. I take a deep breath in and expel the negative thoughts through my exhale. I then inhale life with a positive phrase (it takes practice, but it works).

My Water Prayer: Help me have control over my mind.

What is your Naked Thought or reflection?

_____

_____

_____

_____

_____

Naked With My Heart

Write down a negative thought that keeps recycling. What will you do the next time that thought arises?

_____

_____

_____

_____

_____

_____

Water Prayer:

_____

_____

Idea: Find someone you can trust to hold you accountable. Tell them one of your destructive thoughts and have a weekly conversation about what you did to defeat it. It will start to lose power over you once it's in the light.

Ariston C.M

Un-boxing God

While we would like to think we know all there is about God, His character, His ways, and His uniqueness, I'm afraid we don't. God works with us on an individual basis according to our needs and His desires for us at the time. We come to God naked, needing to be clothed. Clothed with righteousness, dignity, and a strong sense of who we are and how we are to serve Him. That is something that takes time. To serve God we only need a willing heart, we don't need to be perfect before we come to Him. In fact, He works best when we are blemished. Why is that, you may ask? It is because we come to Him not knowing anything, not trying to be in control, but in need of instruction, guidance, love, and fulfillment.

God is gracious and loving, full of mercy. In all actuality, we don't know how He's going to deal with us. Why? Because God deals with the heart, out of our understanding, knowledge, and experiences. With this being said, it is impossible to know how and in which ways He will move or judge. This is why we can't box Him in. God speaks to me in various ways. I have never heard an audible voice. However, He has spoken to me in unconventional ways through music, pictures, signs, feelings, etc. I know a person that says God speaks to them through fancy cars. It may sound silly to you, but it works for that individual. We will not understand and is not for us to do so, because it is not our life or our journey. We need to understand who God is to us, in the context of our journey.

Naked With My Heart

It is my hope that you have learned or seen something about yourself in these seven days. I pray that you have felt God's presence and are ready to continue on your way to a deep and meaningful relationship with Him. This is not the end, but the beginning of something great!

I want to hear from you. What did God reveal to you in these seven days? Have you gained better control over your mind or situation? Do you feel closer to Him? I have several ways you can contact me. They are listed below.

Please provide me with honest feedback. This is important as it will allow me to improve as a writer, and of course it will give me ideas about future books. I would like to thank you for getting my devotional, it means a lot to me. I hope I have touched your heart in some way. If you have not had the chance to get my other book, *The Courage to Dance Again: Finding Purpose in Your Pain*, it's on Amazon. Get your copy!

It would make me smile if I heard from you. Ways to connect with me:

Email: connect@loveariston.com

Website: LoveAriston.com

Of course I'm on social media...

Facebook: Ariston CM

Instagram & Twitter: imsoariston

Hugs & Kisses, Ariston!

Ariston C.M

About the Author

Ariston C.M. was born in and currently resides in Ohio. She is an entrepreneur and has a Master's in Christian Education, Diploma of Theology in Black Church Studies, Child Development Associate Credential (CDA) and working toward a second Master's in Clinical Counseling. Her challenges as a child ultimately inspired her to start a non-profit organization that currently addresses the needs of at-risk youth and those with developmental disabilities. Ariston has developed a multitude of programs and taught various workshops. She is a speaker both nationally and internationally. She is passionate about empowering individuals to live beyond their pain and walk in their purpose. In her free time, she enjoys nature, traveling, and spending quality time with her children. Ariston's husband is a pastor and they have a church in Ghana. Ariston has two other books, *The Courage to Dance Again: Finding Purpose in Your Pain* and *Poetry's Love Song*. Both are available on Amazon.

www.ingramcontent.com/pod-product-compliance
Lightning Source LLC
Chambersburg PA
CBHW070739020526
44118CB00035B/1765